is an internationally-acclaimed independent publishing house, literary journal, radio show, and arts organisation dedicated to the celebration of music in all of its forms. Half Mystic Press, our publishing arm, releases three to five books of prose, poetry, and experimental work per year—invocations of love, wildness, and uncertainty, the heartbeat of humanity set to a 4/4 time signature, expanding and redefining unsung narratives, sharp and lamenting, eyes on the horizon. For more information, books similar to this one, and submission guidelines, please visit www.halfmystic.com.

Praise for Hag

"A sweeping, visceral, and brilliant collection of shape-shifting poems that applies Tamara Jobe's mastery of from to the liminal space between the sacred and profane. Jobe transforms every inch of the body into a landscape to probe and surrender. The subversions in this slow incantatory spell are hard to forget. One leaves this book with the pulse of the 'open-eyed snake poem' lit wide, inside."

—*Alina Stefanescu,* author of *Every Mask I Tried On*

"Painfully relatable and beautifully written, *Hag* is at once discreet and devastating, an honest and raw glimpse into nature, femininity, and humanity."

—*Lynsey Morandin,* editor-in-chief of Hypertrophic Press

"Tamara Jobe speaks with the tongue of the ancient priestess. *Hag* is a tome of the unbearable, the lost, hidden and beautiful. It is the 'feral hymn / sung only in the dark', evoking the long-lost, or present, goddess. Jobe writes with a vulnerability so rare it alters the reader and brings them to the edge of the world where they meet, truthfully and irrevocably, themselves at the altar."

—*Haley Wooning*, author of *mothmouth*

FIRST PRINTING, AUGUST 2019
HALF MYSTIC PRESS
www.halfmystic.com

COPYRIGHT © TAMARA JOBE, 2019

EDITED *by* DANIE SHOKOOHI
DESIGNED *by* TOPAZ WINTERS

ALL RIGHTS RESERVED

We think you know the drill already. Except for quotation of short passages for the purpose of critical review, no part of this publication may be reproduced in any form or by any means, electronic or print, including photocopying, recording, or by any information storage and retrieval system, without the prior permission in writing from the author and Half Mystic Press. Don't steal art, okay? Authors need to eat too.

ISBN-13: 978-1-948552-06-6
ISBN-10: 1-948552-06-X

HAG

Tamara Jobe

A
Half Mystic Press
Publication

For the women in my life

Creation

in dreams, he finally finds a place
for the stories. the feathery ones

about a spider god whose web
spindled the world into being.

and the claw-and-tooth ones
in which the first coyote pack

hounds and kills the hare, makes a pact
with man, woeful howling

after dusk spills blue across
the plain. sometimes,

the witches place the bone,
the acorn, and the rosemary

into the fire and chant a new tongue
for the people.

in dreams, he must give the stories
a voice. in waking,

they become feral hymns,
sung only in the dark.

Holy

nothing is holy
but still I breathe in the simple pleasure of green air
on the road to Big Sur, Holy Road to Seaward Shore—

California like an overripe plum, pear-grained and
too-juicy; what memories could we make
before the morning? what thing could I not utter because
against the waves her face was a nymph's?

I look back on the old photographs
and all are grayer
than I remember.

She

I.

I scrape together poems with wisp and smoke,
green apple tart hint:

cerebellum-poem;
open-eyed snake poem;
fog-of-war poem and orchard trenched
poem—

gnashed equine teeth, split
down the middle; calcium-covered poems
scooped up

II.

When mother that I knew best laid her
silken side along the Ozarks,
I do but know you:

heavy seasalt womb and cracked
side of goddess; I at last veer
and touch her wings, Mother
sweet-but-sad champagne color around
every childhood polaroid. we hold
together, together *to get her*

III.

my many vice-fissured bird poem:

the crow that tears out her own feathers
and cannot put back. Full as she is

of female and mind and chasm
never knowing where to put anything

anymore

IV.

I laid myself naked on the long frenzied road
to Mexico—

let ravage be from the men with oiled caps
whose pockets jingled with coin and eyes
burned holes under my feet

V.

She. *She:*
she rises with her limbs and worry and knowing—

She lays jasmine flower on her white sill; it is 1956
and her apartment smells of citrus and starch. French
moon hangs heavy like a swallow's nest in staunch winter.

No one understands why she stains
every fine napkin with ink or what madness
feeds her muteness.

VI.

Frida, Billie, Victoria, Virginia;

echo back your howling—what have you become
in those many years beyond the grave?

What dual-world travelers are you,
what wood and ocean greets your force—

VII.

Girl. followed home by strangers,
pretty girl with root-chunks ripped from her scalp,
child resenting the trouble to retain

the memory at all. I don't retain you.

VIII.

lightning-bug poem flung from a Midwestern rooftop,
hot cats on a sizzling roof, fiddler on the roof,

I see teenaged-self omitted somewhere, displaced,
put her laughing on the roof. In the backdrop
juts a cotton gin,
the whiteballs soft mounds of sinewy forgiveness.

Merge

held by warm water: am I loved yet?
fed, clothed, blistered, shod. open mouths for air,
   little glimpses of heart beating, pulped, in my hands. are you listening?   because the voices of many children are forgotten.   get out of bed.
concrete floor, orange juice, the fissures on my fingers. stop singing.   be silent as a dead lamb, puddled about in afterbirth.   am I loved?   the world goes silent and dark. the language of the night carries me home, her arms cool and strong.

Dreams

your hawk-eyes find me,
reave into my side
as a flock of wounded animals.
your voice, sharp as a new star:
*where are you? the sky is pushing itself
apart,* as if I am expected
to encircle the universe with my small arms
and stitch it back together.
I do not have sinews to spare.

you look at me, empty-eyed,
as if waiting to be fed.

God(dess)

what does it feel like?

    when the day breaks & it tastes of   tangerines bleeding hearts an untouched honeysuckle a land purified by fire.   all that lives here is the sun and lines upon lines of aspen.

when a river finds its way after eons of struggle.   petrified shells   fish losing its scales trees refusing to open.

    when she says to me, *jump, feet first. you don't need permission to live.*

Truth Emerges From Her Well

    amiss
    amassing the amorous,

a gala of riddles, arranged and rearranged like the father of
his father and his father   and so on through
a gallery of portraits swathed in grey

I am becoming what I have seen in your clandestine
mirror, a story of the oak and rowan, leavened. I am
followed by an oracle of kings. memories erased, a woman
with my face rises like truth screaming from the well of
discontent

Blackwater

*I live in a small pale house / a moment's march /
from the beach / my day is growing near / and here I
find no peace at all / and here I find no peace at all*

—Aldous Harding, "No Peace At All"

At night I feel the sea burning in me.

Beyond the island, its milky hues solidifying in lunar planes under my feet, I search for stinging things on the pier: a pair of trampled glasses, all hushed and rubbed down, lost girl sight; petrified starfish, cracked down the middle and lighter than air; an abandoned boat shoe, men's size ten, a tassel missing and frayed, as if bitten, as if decayed.

I collect these talismans,
stripped, raw, sick with seasalt and heavy,

a waiting womb
suddenly full of thumbs.

Is it the water that burns? Her darkness that deepens
in refusals; worry stones; a black bag of earth.

My feet carry me to the house,
carry my thumb womb,
carry an entire sea, burning.

Soon, the day, with its promises,
its flat arias, its limp and its questions.
I press against the front door,
reach to open it. I won't say what hurts.

Veil

the wolves in their husked folds
will dance. I am silent;

Her gaze has fallen and I have emptied my hands
of dirt. I am not touched (I am not

changed). skies brindle against the turning
season; She balks behind Her veil.

men fret. they wonder why they cannot
hold more. why they cannot

eat my hair and wear my skin. their eyes
heavy like plated coins.

I turn my face, silent: what is there to say?
I watch my mother who watches

the wolves whine & prize, bare their tufted necks
to one another in sacrifice.

Silence

I have bruised my being for the world.
Stared into the faces of gods and found them
    with nothing to say.

Silent as sparrows with wings caught in wire,
    hanging / hung.

I have held my breath for so long that my lungs
    bleed. Frozen, timeless, mouth as wide as tundra.
    Every living thing here
    has gone blue.

I see what the world means when it says
"Tell me a story." Don't speak unless
it's what you want to hear. What you can swallow /

what you can fit into your mouth / what you can vomit
back up.

II.

Hag

I bristle on you.
I put my whole being into the nothing of my name.

> Wander the tongue of lowland
> until my skin surfaces
> into mirror. Raucous. Cascade.

And I chew and I chew and I chew
and I spit and I say "hag."
I have that word, too.
I'll have all the words that blister.

> I say "hag" because you forbid it.
> Because witches climb walls.
> Because you clap my mouth shut
> & burn holes under my feet.
> Because the wifehood of my land
> weds itself.

River

the hand has pulled me
from myself;

all I remember is the feeling of water,
a tide ebbing, two waves

being waves, splitting.
she says, "this is all

you are: a fistful of water.
you are the shape

of the one that holds you."

Hunger

At night we walk the fields and loom together.

We dip our feet into dark streams,
murmuring discoveries.

> Stitching our sides closed,
> our mouths closed,
> our eyes open.

We see hunger
washing her stricken hands,
slender, vexed. She tells us
not to blink. Hardly to breathe.

> The smell of burning things
> on our tongues.

We molt under the moon,
twin moths cannibalizing their wings.
We flex together, nebulous,
imagining a dawn
we no longer have to feed.

One we can peer into and say,
"find another."

Creature

Say, there's a star.
And under that star there are

a hundred hearts: twining and veining
together. And under those hearts are

hands whose cells remember other cells.
Hands clasped and pulped,

dovetailed. And these hearts are ripped
from chest cavities but home

in other hands. Because stars sing to stars,
because hands hold hearts,

a delicate glory, life for a life.
Our heavy sky is painted red.

So much red that bursts the sky.

Salt

another word for *salt*:

the iridescent brine plucked
from a mare's eyelashes;

a cask full of moon, pulled-to,
tucked under the tongue;

and between your fingers,
a benediction, soft

as robin's egg; to hold
this reflection of life

in a calcified shell.
break it to pieces, crush

the tawny shards
under your heel.

you have another word for *salt*.
another word for *alive*,

nudged into meaning, safe for later,
as you need it. to taste.

Heft

big woman with a backwards glare:

>add a pulse, two steps,
>a shuffle in the grime of life
>subtract a pound of flesh

big woman who looks back while looking forward:

>two eyes to look, to be seen,
>self-hands to carry her
>lief as the sea, coral-full

big woman roves:

>not too much, not too deep,
>learn what you can in secret
>speak what you can in secret

save a little,
learn to be more whole than anyone
scowl into the sun, transfixed in green:

protect everything warm,
everything left to lose

Sanguine

after Dhrit

i've found parts of meaning along the scales on your back:
i count their color. i testify to you: *elderberry blue,
dampened in the evergreen.* strange how small you become
in memories.

    what is left of our strength? how many times have
we said, *things will get better*—and do they? sisters watch
sisters die, bury secret things behind fences. intuit crickets
in the wet soil when summer gets too long. i cut away the
fat, preparing dinner in fading light.

    no one speaks in this house. hallways labor. silence
gloats in the throats of sinners.

    what remains of you? i follow your trail of scales,
offering myself. your skin glows translucent, hollow as
embryo. inside you run blood-red. you radiate the heaviest
light.

Milk

      In the morning I think of the land Yahweh
      promised Abraham:
of honey. Of milk. Sweet things nestled reedy along the
river.

      Some mornings to remember a future death: did
he mount Palatine Hill, thinking of her lilac hair? Her
skin

      thick, a silvered cup of mare's milk
for swallowing fear.

      Small chukar tends to her younglings.
She sips from morning dew // watches for phantoms

      beyond the mouthy sky. And with blank face, I
      pour milk
on her paltry grave.

Green / Gold

Father, I am you. I am of you. Half-blind,
> Half sorry for your sight. I do not have what
> you have. Your beating heart softer than any
> heart. You know what I will never know:
> Father, I am of you.

Those hands are strong, but not stronger than any hand. What you grip becomes you, part of you: I watch the smoke in the pearlescent sky settle like dust in your eyes. You breathe. I look at you and you look at me and you are good. You are good. You are golden and green and take your place higher in the sky than any sky; I carry you; I am you; I am of you. You are of me.

The world blinks. You smile behind the glass door, tell me *I'm here*.

Destined

I once plotted out my love:

>wayward interloper, burdened with fresh lilacs
>and wafting patchouli rose. Haunted
>by some serene fever, content, bent forward
>& manufacturing hunger.

I would hold her close.
I would blink, heavy-lidded, our bluish bodies
>layered on sheets slicker than love,
>smoother than bullfrogs leaping
>to their muddy holes.

I would raise fires for her: hunting & pulling & scraping together
every last fading story,
every tongue of black smoke,
and she would smile

kiss my eyes

and only then would we materialise for each other:

pine needles stuck to our skin,
a new & long language birthed for us,
sticky & restless,
satisfaction clenched in its angry fists.

Void Hymn

I.

The wound ripens. Against the backdrop
    of slippery greens I shed secrets
    to my four-legged wards.
    They blink wide-eyed and silent,
    send watchful desert prayers
    to ancestors of my ancestors
    that they carried.

II.

Civilization—libraries, mosques, mosaic
    mindfulness. Cicero's toddling
    chariot carries him to his next
    engagement, lightly sweating
    voice lifts to a voracious sun.

III.

She smiles at me from behind the counter,
        clutching a bundle of sage.
        Her crystal chimes paint the quiet
        in array—drake's-neck, pervenche.
        An occult child topples toy pillars
        representing a temple.

IV.

The soul lurches and slogs,
        I (some form of I) ride wingless
        clouds to some empty city.
        The woods are burning and
        smoke clogs the air. She
        asks me, *do you remember*
        the color of sky?

I can't say that I do. The stars
blacken. God turns loose
Aurora's luminous skirts.

III.

Heathen

It's true that I've pulled you out of me.
This way, when the shower leaks,
when the cats haven't eaten & you wonder
why the walls are painted red, I can grin
and grimace. (The library will get
finished; I'll burn that sage bundle you hate seeing because
it reminds you that I'm different
these days.) I'm different these days.
I don't see worship. I don't see *God* or *Holy Spirit*
or those things that shape up the framework; that nail bits
of you together until without them,
you drift like singed matches down the gutter.

Forgive me.

I curse your sweet things. Bite
my tongue numb. I like to roll in mire
because it's easier than the alternative:
peeling myself from you like an old skin,
and then: soft, pink, & blank.

Telling myself
it's good.

Ghost

I've waited until now
to tear to pieces
this little bed of styrofoam—

        ripple glittering clouds of snow
          touching everything with its gluttonous palms

      My head grows heavy as a melon,
        a blue bottle. A parting smile. A secret door

    fluttering shut—

I view her, beloved,
from tomorrow:
a wind-reddened face,
moonshaped. Immense.
Immovable. A glancing-back
glimmer on her shoulders.
(The never of her dark,
lidded eyes.)

Ragged Tooth, Ragged Claw

You witch,
you vague-shaped, all your limbs aflame,

you blacked-out & tarry vagrant:
pillar of mercury.

Like a mountain, V-shaped,
draped & swum. Swinging,

smoke across your eyes.
Perched upon a pyre,

a seed to be wrenched
from the grouse's mouth:

how many teeth in your head?
More than mine, more than me.

Your thighs buckling latitudes,
windy bridge between.

Climbing these walls I'll shade night.
I'll wobble & gobble like stars

huntering blue plains: from dirt
& earth I'll pull you to me

until your face is a face molded,
agleam. Witch in the stream.

Easy

I'll consume it over again, flawless
word. Shall I? Dare I
      gnash it up in my mouth
& spit it out into the shape of *girl*? I wonder,
      does it please you?

Hungry is the way I speak. The accent of my mother's
      mother, thinking growing up meant *better*.
Better meant this destiny: fulfilling a purpose
      with eyes. Scars. Hands. Tongue on skin,
      safe but for the back of me.

But I say even with this body,
      what is there to prove? With bloody sheets,
      immaculate, carefully measured—I'm at ease in
      this.

In this I open my mouth
Say *crone*. Say *belonging*.
Pull every burr, spear, blade to my chest
& feel no pain.

Bear

or: *to be borne.*
        to carry the weight, or
              / to be carried /
to carry a heavy silence, sea-wide
to wade into,   to buoy earth's nape

     to lift it up
     above some glassy surface,
     and then to sink yourself:
     a slippery gasp, until everywhere
     an empty space

Bloom

after Eleanor Gray

I am born of this:

> aisles of mirage, draped in slick cur,
> burrs upon the veil: each forlorn call
> like wet feathers of geese.

I feed the mirrored image:

> gutted fish scraped from the river's
> siltsides, waves of green, the many lush
> & curdled sheep wafting in thick heather.

Each day I look, my gaze a new gaze:

> what eyes may look back?
> Now that I am just a dark coppery bloom,
> a warm blush of blood,

a feverish stain
smudged away
by some savage caress

Suffocate

I'm in bed. This non-hour. This gauzy morning dusk.
    I'm in bed with the devil. Darken your eyes—
nothing you can't see (haven't seen). My lips form *spiritus sancti*,
        marked by that black night. Better latch your
        door.
I'm in bed at this non-hour, hazy glazey gauzy twilight,
    I'm at your side. I'm in you, in me, no satisfaction
comes from forgetting. Lie down, side by side.
    Fall asleep in that deep dark ground.

Sad Song

In a thousand years

>you are the petrified bark sleeve
>now become some final stone
>glittering somewhere in the summer
>heat;   and I am there,

a glimpse of life, overturned,

>cradled in a bed of moss.
>The birds go frail, creaking into some
>sad song. The kind of song
>you'd listened to centuries ago

alone at your desk, or bed, or kitchen table

>with ash falling from your fingers,
>thinking you were alone. As you were.
>As was everyone. Blinking your little
>solitary flashlight,

searching for signs of life.

Grief

This is love's aftermath,
when you wade out: brave // watchless,
    into the shallow murk of riverwater,
        mouthful of sand // my merchant of hours.

There is a kind of dusk
    to your beyond. A kind of weightless chimera,
        buying all that I have // measuring spokes.

I cannot wade to you.
    Cannot wonder what brumy mouth
        speaks me out of being // what stakes me
    out of longing.

IV.

Revolve

The sun rises & sets
and there's not much to it except

the in-between; grey morning & a night
crowing hungry in the dark. I make

dotted lines that never connect, crawl
back into my cave. Never have I been

so lonely. I am always waiting
for something to happen. I look out

and the sun & sky & every hollow
turns pink. Maybe this is the light

I never knew I needed. This light
reminding me of what I am.

Dust

beyond the ledge, I see the bodies molded in concrete,
commas, dividing lines between numbers calculating their
own worth. i look into the face of a man,
vacantly bruised; his fingers curled like weeping doves. he
tucks a shadow into his mouth, forever the gasping
expression of choke. he is naked, granular & grey, dust-
covered. his shoulder is wedged between a woman's
hip and horn of rhinoceros, and i think, *how must the gods
temper their work?*—nothing can stay,
not even anguish. i kiss them, their inconspicuous wrists,
swallow spit, suddenly thirsty.

Wolfskin

into the moonshadow, betweenfingers shadow
       (and chin   and toes   and lobes)
     uncarried i am rove into rove, the night has
     made a hungry beast of me,
and she has carried for too long
the promised, the promiseless,
the key of wintering   in August
an untimely drop   of all she
hoped to remember

     and i cannot hold   all the years of you
     the years of you in the years of your mother

     too long to take another step,
     her fearful lack of dark

a sistine, she said, a sistine is a pristine thing, a divine
lighting on the face of god—and where does god lie?
god lies in granular clay, god has a mouth full of sand.
god calls her a little wolf. god tugs on the throat of the
wolf. crooked surrender. all our days
are full of blood anyway.

this, too, is simple for you.
this is an egg, uncracked.
this is an afterbirth of
littered lanes. in the lanes
we smoke together, we
dance with our mouths
open, we shed our
skins like eels at the
bottom of the sea,
don't they? don't
they?

        take your victor back, then,
        take your savior back.
        i count your parts, one by
        one. hide myself between
        your fingers. the lines that
        rend your heart: those
        are mine, also.

do we not taste of blood?

    the wolf never touches   the same life twice

Be Round

   The sound of *round* is wide,   everything   says it is
like a mouth.   Full of aplomb.   Full to the brim
   of wine, of ambrosia, of something sweet / savory.

   Everything resounds. Flesh-hipped and avery-starred,
that it is a *she*. S/he. S[he]. An amorphous freckled she,
   or we, or *they*. She brims & bustles & you want her
because she seems to want for nothing.

The Body Is an Evening

The body is an evening,
        russet and ripe,   all sky is skin with a longing call
          and everywhere, in everything,
            feathered with geese winging mournfully.
Green are the hills that loom and loam,   fetching
fragrant cedarwood;   the scent of night is a long one,
swaying to some primordial song.   All along
the ridge, flecked & shimmering like glass,
foxes & forests borrow light.
Evening rolls like a body, cowled,
culling itself until it is
a gray winter field,
                memories of glimmering wheat.

Figs

You're forever needling through me,
        as if it's dark,
        as if it's always beginning,
        as if hunting & catching & tossing
        me back to sea.

I thumb the edges of you,
        your grass-mouth,
        your numb sky,
                plucked through with stars.

We split it down the middle, bitten fighearts,
needle through the tender seed. Every
sticky drop licked from our fingers:
how I recall your mouth—
        laughter descending to the valley,
        light darkening to shadow,
        but sweet
        like figs.

Mama Mull

I eat at the kitchen sink
& think of the oranges
         squares of dark chocolate
         half moons of baby bell cheese
             wrapped in foil;

The gesture of *clean*
& mostly, hands everywhere
flickering domestic shadows
of time moving through you,
         where we're together
         where we're safe
         & still singing

Conjugal

If this is all I can bear
        then I'm a light to be consumed
        I'm a glistening heart beating itself
        into something,
        a real thing.

If this is all I can bear
        then I sit at the edge of breath,
        I look down—I look down
        and all I see is a hazy shell of me
        rubbing its walls raw.

What is there left to say?
            What have I left to destroy?
        If this is all I can bear
            then I'll look up at the blue swell of sky,
close this body, this glittering body that is mine,
        breathe again. Ask to sleep.

Sacral

There is in your face
                every shape of light.

1. No wasteful bloom in the crook of your spine:
   only that it was clean, lupine, some honey to taste.

2. A song is seamless when it is from memory. No edges,
   a kiss of lavender at the temple. A shy kind of held.

3. We recline and reside at the brush of forest,
   spiced cedar.   Brumy bracken under your eyes.

4. The swell of you is what I remember: that
   blurred space between silence & hymn.

Otherkin

After all, I'm very good
at the spooling of emotion,
which gather like twine into

sequential knots, or rootlock
themselves, their waif-bodies,
altogether. I cannot make them out.

Will I not ask myself again
to *wild*. To *toothbear*. Smooth
myself into less-than-human.

Will I not swallow that bitter
pill, wet with void? Do as I am told?
Roll / spool / face-eat?

Phantom

I don't want the flesh
that sits on me. That sits or spits
or is fitted
to bone. Of fish
retiring again and again
to goldwater. Retiring
their dark desire. This milk
this flesh
that grubs. Supples,
pools porous
ekes out. I feel
the aging, heavier as it descends.
Soon, what will remember?
I speak to the black trees
and they do nothing
but shudder. Sway
in my girlish sway.

Woman

I am in a chamber and you are here, too.
I want to tell you I've been ashamed every day of my life.

I dress and rattle my fat, hooks, blend truth away.

I sense you near and can't look you in the eyes.

I have found every night my back is against the wall.
Loneliness is synonymous with *woman*.

My mother never told me what it meant. What I was.
How to believe I deserved more than the space I'm in.

So it is down to this: who waits, who goes on with it,
who walks forward into shadow without looking back.

Acknowledgements

"Truth Emerges From Her Well" was originally published in *Verdancies Journal*.

"Blackwater" was originally published in *What Fresh Witch Is This?*

"Salt" was originally published in *Bird's Thumb*.

About the Author

Tamara Jobe lives in the South, tending horses and writing poems.

www.ingramcontent.com/pod-product-compliance
Lightning Source LLC
Chambersburg PA
CBHW030132100526
44591CB00009B/614